CK

Sounds & Letters 8

KNOWLEDGE BOOKS

tick	sick
duck	clock
rock	sock
back pack	

ck

tick

3

sick

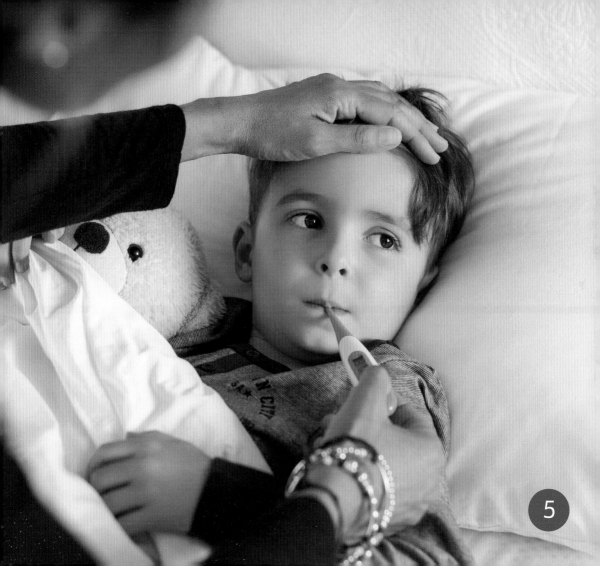

duck

clock

9

rock

sock

13

back pack

tick	sick
duck	clock
rock	sock
back pack	

Knowledge Books and Software
PO Box 50 Sandgate, Queensland 4017 Australia
p. +617-55680288 f. +617-55680277 email: sales@kbs.com.au

First Published 2022
ISBN 9781922516800
Text and editing: Carole Crimeen
Design and layout: Suzanne Fletcher
Publisher: Robert Watts

Series Information: **Sounds and Letters**

Credits
Photographs: Cover © paulaphoto; p. 1 © Nik Merkulov, Lev Kropotov, AlexLMX, Pixabay; p. 3
© PAPound; p. 5 © Rido; p. 7 © Tetiana Leman; p. 9 © mogilami; p. 11 © chittakorn59; p. 13 ©
New Africa; p. 15 © Rajesh Narayanan/Shutterstock.

Phonic support books are a wonderful resource for emergent readers as they encourage independent reading and help students make the link between letters and the sounds they represent.

Have students identify the images on the title page to listen for the sound that they will hear through the book.

Encourage students to point to each word as they read through the book.

ISBN: 9781922516800

9 781922 516800 >

KNOWLEDGE BOOKS

Sounds& Letters